Contents

Skateboarding

▲

Skateboarding pro Bucky Lasek pulls a spectacular move at a vert skateboarding competition in New York City.

Skateboarding is an exciting individual sport. Riders travel at speed on their wheeled skateboards and use them to pull amazing tricks. Skateboarding started out as a way that sea surfers could surf on land – they nailed roller skate wheels to a plank of wood. Now, it's a huge sport with millions of skateboarders worldwide.

Skateboarding can be a truly spectacular sport. But young skateboarders can get just as much of a thrill from learning and performing simple tricks.

Unless you're taking part in a competition, skateboarding has few rules, just important safety tips. This means you can learn in your own time and have the freedom to invent your own moves. Many skateboarders say that the sport is all about freedom.

There are different types of skateboarding. You can just cruise around, using your skateboard as a fun type of transport. Alternatively, you can learn tricks and moves using rails and kerbs in the street or enjoy riding around or on the obstacles in special skateparks.

Vert skateboarding features large ramps, deep bowls and giant pipes. Boarders use these objects to perform incredible feats of agility and timing including leaps, twists and somersaults.

▲ This skateboarder is riding along a metal rail. Sliding and grinding are major parts of street-style skateboarding.

◀ A skateboarder enjoys riding on her skateboard at a skatepark. The front of a board is called the nose and the turned up back is called the kicktail.

Nailing it!

Some skateboarders are happy just riding on their board but most cannot resist the temptation of learning new tricks. Nailing a trick – mastering it, so that you can perform it again and again – is a great challenge and a real thrill.

Patience is crucial. You'll need to work hard and persevere through many failed attempts to nail a trick. Keep at it and ask more experienced skateboarders for tips and advice.

▼ The only thrill equal to the first time you nail a trick is to perform it well in front of your friends. This is the real reward for all the hard work involved.

Performing an ollie

Start to move with your front foot between the middle of the board and the front trucks (see page 10) and your back foot on the tail.

Push the tail of the board down hard onto the floor. As the nose rises, drag your front foot up to the nose of the board and lift your back foot up and forwards.

Keep your bodyweight over the board as you lift your knees up to pull the board up with you as you jump. Use your knees and arms to balance as you land.

Learning to ollie is important, as it is one of the most useful tricks in skateboarding. Knowing how to ollie allows you to jump into the air on your board and is the starting point for other, more complex tricks.

◄

Skate star Vanessa Torres rides a rail during the 2009 X Games competition. Like all pros, Torres puts hundreds of hours into perfecting new moves.

Kit and clothing

Skateboards come in many different models and sizes. All have key parts – from the deck, the large flat surface you ride on, to the trucks that attach the wheels and axles to the deck. When you're buying your first skateboard, get as much advice as you can from experienced skateboarders.

Over time, your skateboard will take a battering so it is important to do pre-ride checks. These include

▼ The underside of a board is covered in a shiny finish, which makes it good for slides (see page 18). Inside each wheel are steel balls called bearings. These help the wheels to run smoothly.

Truck baseplate

Truck bolts

Hanger

Wheel facts

Skateboard wheels are made of a material called urethane. Wheels come in different sizes and some wheels are harder than others. Softer wheels are used on roads and rough ground. Most vert skaters use larger, harder wheels.

Wheels often wear on the outer edges. You can turn them round to extend their life.

checking that the truck bolts and nuts holding the wheels on the axle are secure, that the

deck isn't split and that the four wheels run freely.

Skateboarders prefer to wear loose-fitting clothing so that they can move freely. They wear skate shoes which have a flat sole which grips the skateboard well. Skateboarding is a risky business and a helmet and joint pads are essential.

▼ This skateboarder is adjusting the tightness of the truck bolts on the underside of her board. Looser trucks allow you to turn more easily, but make a board harder to ride at high speed.

▼ This boy rides a skateboard ramp wearing a comfortable, well-fitting helmet. He has strapped on pads to protect his knees and elbows should he fall.

Skateboarding stars

Top skateboarders such as Tony Hawk, Ryan Sheckler, Lyn-Z Adams Hawkins and Vanessa Torres are professional stars, paid to perform at competitions and exhibitions. They put their names to ranges of equipment, clothing and games. They have fans all over the world.

However, most professional skateboarders are not highly paid.

They may receive small amounts of sponsorship money from equipment makers or win prize money at small skateboard competitions.

Pro performances

In 2005, pro skateboarder Danny Way sped down a giant ramp before leaping over the gigantic Great Wall of China.

In 2000, Richie Carrasco performed 142 360-degree turns on his skateboard in a row. It is still a dizzying world record!

▼ Cara-Beth Burnside competes at the 2009 X Games in California. A female skateboarding pioneer, she was the first woman to have her own line of skate shoes.

▲ Tony Hawk, the world's most famous skateboarder, at the unveiling of his waxwork at Madame Tussauds in Hollywood. His home has skate ramps outside and special floors inside so he can skate indoors!

Skateboarding stars perform moves that wow crowds, but they only nail these moves after years of hard work. They take risks and push themselves to the limit to learn daring new moves and thrill spectators when they perform in competition. This can lead to injuries. Tony Hawk, for example, has broken his elbow, ribs and pelvis. Other star skateboarders have had similar lists of injuries, but all say that they sport is worth the risks they have to take.

Starting off

▲ There are two stances in skateboarding. Regular stance (shown here on the right) is with your left foot forward. Goofy stance (here on the left) is with your right foot forward.

Skateboarders start by learning how to ride a skateboard in a straight line. First of all, they must work out whether they prefer to ride with their right or left foot forward. This is called their stance.

Once on a board, skateboarders concentrate on their balance and control. They bend their knees to create human shock absorbers that are able to soak up small bumps and dips. They lift their head up and hold their arms out to help them balance.

Skateboarders perform gentle turns by leaning and pressing on the edges of the board. To make a frontside turn they press down with their toes on the edge of the board to make it veer in a gentle curve.

▲ This skateboarder pushes off, pawing the ground with his back foot. He puts both feet on the board to ride it, turning his front foot so it is across the board. He takes his back foot off the board and drags it on the ground to slow down and stop.

To make more sudden turns, press on the kicktail to lift the nose of your board up and to swivel it to the left or the right. These moves are called kickturns. You can perform repeated quick kickturns to the left and right to move forward. This simple trick is called a tic-tac.

◀

This rider presses down on his board's kicktail to lift the nose off the ground.

Flips and grabs

Once you can get plenty of height, known as air, on your ollies, you can start learning other tricks. These include flips during which the board spins 360 degrees through the air as you perform an ollie.

The kickflip, shown in the pictures below, is the first flip most skateboarders learn. Heelflips are similar to kickflips but the heel of the front foot is used to flip the board over.

▼ For this kickflip, the skateboarder performs an ollie then slides his front foot off the front and side of the board close to where the front bolts are. This is what makes the board flip.

▲ This skateboarder performs an indy grab in mid-air. He leans forward and uses his rear hand (his right) to grab the board between his feet.

With both heel and kickflips, riders watch their board carefully whilst in the air. As soon as they see the top of the deck coming over, they plant their feet on the board and brace themselves, bending their knees for landing.

Grabs are moves in which the rider holds or touches the board during a trick. These are often performed in the middle of an aerial trick, such as an ollie, or as a skateboarder flies off the top of a ramp. The indy grab, shown on this page, is a common first grab to learn. A mute grab is similar to the indy but uses the front hand instead of the back.

Flip facts

The kickflip was invented by Rodney Mullen in the early 1980s. In the late 1980s, Mullen won 34 out of the 35 skateboarding competitions he entered.

Some very skilled skateboarders are able to perform a quadflip by flipping their board through four complete turns before landing on it.

17

Grinds and slides

For many street skating moves you ride your board but not on its wheels. Skateboarders use the bottom of the deck for slides and ride on the metal trucks to perform grinds. Grinds and slides are often performed on narrow metal rails or kerbs.

To slide you can either use the middle of the board, between the two trucks, or one of its ends. To perform a tail slide, for example, you slide along a rail or obstacle only on the tail part of your skateboard. Keeping well balanced is crucial so you need to use your arms and small shifts of bodyweight to keep stable as you slide along.

▼ To perform this boardslide trick the rider balances with his weight equally over each foot. The front truck is over the rail or kerb and the skateboard slides along the middle of the bottom of the deck.

▲ For a 50-50 grind the skateboarder jumps up and onto the rail and rides with his weight based equally over the middle of both trucks.

▲ To perform a nose grind the skater hops up onto the obstacle so that he rides along on just the front truck with the board's tail in the air.

There are many different types of grinds including 50-50s and nose grinds (shown in the photos on this page). In a feeble grind the board grinds along only on the rear truck with the front of the board hanging over the toeside edge of the obstacle.

Skateparks and safety

If you visit a skatepark you'll find it's equipped with plenty of fun skateboarding obstacles to enjoy. These include ramps, snake runs – twisting downhill slopes – and funboxes. Funboxes are angled blocks with small ramps on each side from which you can pull jumps, ollies and other moves.

At a skatepark you must wear a helmet, follow all the park's rules, and treat other skateboarders with respect. This includes not hogging a ramp, rail or funbox when there's a queue, and not sitting on an obstacle. You should check the way ahead is clear before riding.

▼ This skateboarder grabs his board as he reaches the top of a tall half-pipe in a skatepark. A skatepark's furniture, such as half-pipes and ramps, is great fun to ride on.

Skateparks and ramps

The first skatepark opened in 1976 in Florida in the United States. Since that time, hundreds have been built.

The SMP park in China is the world's largest skatepark, It's bigger than 20 basketball courts and has a giant 50m-wide vert ramp.

Pro skateboarder Bob Burnquist built his own giant skateboard ramp over 20m high and about 90m long. Riders can reach speeds of over 70km/h whizzing down its slopes.

Help anyone in difficulty and do not put yourself and others at risk by trying out tricks that are far beyond your ability.

It's vital to put safety first whether you are skating in a skatepark or elsewhere. Never skateboard in the rain as you lose all the grip you need to ride safely.

An important part of skateboarding safely is knowing when a trick is going wrong, and how and when to bail, or leave the skateboard. For example, if skaters have to bail when they're skating in a bowl or half pipe (see page 22), they can use a knee slide to travel down and stop on the flat part.

▼ This skateboarder knows he has to bail from his board and performs a knee slide. He steps off the board with his front foot, bends and lands on his knee pads, sliding down the ramp safely.

Vert skating

Vert skating is a thrilling type of skateboarding in which riders use large pieces of equipment to reach a vertical or almost vertical position. These include bowl shapes with high walls and big U-shaped objects called half pipes. Vert skaters also use pairs of large ramps, which are often placed so that they face each other.

The area where a pipe or bowl goes from being flat and level to curving upwards is called the transition. Beginners build up experience by riding the transitions and level parts, getting a feel for the changes in speed and balance needed.

▼ To drop in, a rider places all of his board except the tail over the edge with his body weight over his back foot holding the tail in place. He places his front foot over the front trucks and crouches as he leans gently forwards. Releasing the weight off the tail, the board will dip down until its wheels grip the ramp.

▲ This skateboarder is building up speed and momentum in a half pipe by pumping. He crouches and then straightens his legs as he rises up the slopes of the pipe.

As riders improve their skill and build confidence, they can start increasing their speed back and forth so that they rise to the top of the bowl or pipe, called the lip. There, they can perform simple tricks such as axle stalls, shown in the picture on the left. To perform a tail stall, riders stop on the lip of a pipe or bowl by putting their weight over the tail of the board.

◀ To pull an axle stall you make a kick turn just before you reach the top of the ramp. The two trucks ride along the lip of the ramp.

Getting big air

▲
This skateboarder has ridden up a small ramp at good speed and then jumped off it to gain plenty of air. His legs are bent and his body balanced, ready to perform a trick or to brace himself for a solid landing.

Experienced skateboarders are good at building enough speed to soar high above the lip of a bowl or pipe. This is known as getting big air.

Once above the lip, top skateboarders can pull spectacular tricks which can amaze audiences. These include rotations (turns in the air) before landing. One popular move is the McTwist, named after its inventor, Mike McGill. Skateboarders grab their board as they fly into the air, then make one and a half complete rotations and a backflip so that they are facing back down the ramp.

▲ This skateboarder pulls a great frontside air, grabbing his board and twisting it round.

There are simpler above the lip tricks, too. These include frontside airs in which riders grab the toe side of the board and make a half turn in the air before landing back on the ramp or pipe facing forwards. When a skateboarder finishes a trick and lands riding backwards, it is called a fakie.

Many aerial moves involve turns and grabs. To perform a cannonball, for example, the rider grabs the nose of the board with the front hand and the tail with the back hand. Another simpler move is the nose grab, during which riders hold the front of the board in the air.

▲ Dan Cesar Pardinho leaves his board as he performs a grab during a vert competition in Brazil. You need great timing and lots of practice to perform great vert moves.

The world of skateboarding

Skateboarders often meet up to trade tricks and moves. These events are known as jams and some have developed into major events with bands playing and appearances by some of the top skateboarding stars.

Pro skateboarders compete at major skateboarding contests held all over the world. They also give individual exhibitions of their skills to audiences.

Competitions exist for freestyle skateboarding, riding street courses and performing vert routines on ramps and half pipes. Judges award vert competitors marks based on style, the height they gain above the ramp or pipe, the difficulty of their tricks and how many of their tricks they manage to combine together.

▲ Nelson Mosikili grinds his board along a rail during the first ever Skateboarding World Championships in 2009.

▲ Lyn-Z Adams Hawkins first rode a skateboard when she was just 18 months old. She won the women's vert competition at the X Games in 2007 and the ISF World Championships vert competition in 2009.

Skateboarding is a star attraction at many extreme sports contests including the Gravity Games and the X Games, which began in 1995, as well as dedicated competitions such as the Etnies European Skateboarding Championships.

In 2009, the International Skateboarding Federation organised the first ever World Championship of Skateboarding in Boston in the United States.

Vanessa Torres won the women's park competition for street and Lyn-Z Adams Hawkins won the women's vert event.

Skateboarding prizes

In 2008, Andy Macdonald won his 15th medal at the X Games. No other competitor at the event has won more medals than this.

At the 2003 X Games, Ryan Scheckler became the youngest ever X Games winner. He was just 13 years old. In 2009, he won the ISF World Championship of Skateboarding.

Where next?

These websites and books will help you find out and learn more about skateboarding.

http://yousk8.net/
This site has hundreds of videos of skateboarding sent in by amateurs, including lots of tips and tricks.

http://skateboard.about.com/
This website is packed with skateboarding news, hints on looking after equipment and tips for tricks.

http://www.ukskate.org.uk/
The website of the United Kingdom Skateboarding Association includes a brilliant calendar of competitions, jams and other skateboarding events.

http://www.hdskate.com/skateboarding-articles/
The Heyday Skateboarding website has lots of trick tips and articles for new skateboarders as well as some cool video clips.

http://www.kidsturncentral.com/topics/sports/dewteamprofiles.htm
Read profiles of leading skateboarders at this website.

http://www.tonyhawk.com/
Tony Hawk's official website is full of excellent videos, photos and trick tips.

Books
Skateboarding: Landing The Basic Tricks – Ryan Stutt. A&C Black, 2009.
Written by a skateboard magazine editor, this book contains lots of information on learning to ride and nailing simple tricks.

Extreme Sports: Skateboarding – Ben Powell. Raintree 2003
A good beginner's guide to skateboarding.

Skateboarding – Clive Gifford. Dorling Kindersley, 2006.
Tricks are explained using colourful graphics and photography.

Skateboarding words

air to leave the ground by jumping or performing a move such as an ollie

bailing to move away clear of your board when a skateboarding move goes wrong and you start to fall

dropping in the main way in which people enter a skateboarding bowl or half pipe, from the top

fakie riding backwards on your skateboard

grabs using one or both of your hands to hold the board during a move

grinds moves in which a skateboarder slides along a rail or kerb riding on the skateboard's metal trucks

half pipe a large, U-shaped device on which skateboarders can skate up and down and pull tricks

lip the top edge of a bowl, ramp or half-pipe

ollie a move in which you use your feet to pull the skateboard up into the air

slides moves in which you use the bottom side of your skateboard deck to slide along a rail, kerb or another piece of skatepark furniture

stance the way you position your body on a skateboard and whether your left or right foot is furthest forward

transition the part of a skateboard ramp or pipe which takes a skateboarder from riding on the level to travelling upwards

Index